Library and Information Service

Library materials must be returned on or before the last date stamped or fines will be charged at the current rate. Items can be renewed online, by telephone, letter or personal call unless required by another borrower. For hours of opening and charges see notices displayed in libraries.

Lewisham Library
199-201 Lewisham High Street
London SE13 6LG
Tel: 020 8314 9800
lewishamlibrary@lewisham.gov.uk
www.lewisham.gov.uk/libraries
24hr telephone renewals: **03333 704 700**

A MONKEY AT THE WINDOW
SELECTED POEMS

قردٌ على الشباك
قصائد مختارة

by Al-Saddiq Al-Raddi

الصَّادق الرضي

Translated by Sarah Maguire and Mark Ford

*with Atef Alshaer, Rashid El Sheikh,
Sabry Hafez and Hafez Kheir*

poetry
translation
centre

BLOODAXE BOOKS

Poems © Al-Saddiq Al-Raddi
Translations © Sarah Maguire and Atef Alshaer, Rashid El Sheikh,
Sabry Hafez and Hafiz Kheir
Translations © Mark Ford and Hafiz Kheir
Introduction © Sabry Hafez
Introduction © Sarah Maguire

ISBN: 978 1 78037 272 3

First published in 2016 by
Bloodaxe Books Ltd
Eastburn
South Park
Hexham
Northumberland NE46 1BS

in association with
The Poetry Translation Centre Ltd
Tileyard Studios
12 Tileyard Road
London N7 9AH

www.bloodaxebooks.com
www.poetrytranslation.org

Supported using public funding by
**ARTS COUNCIL
ENGLAND**

CONTENTS

'Songs of Solitude': The Poetry of Al-Saddiq Al-Raddi

SABRY HAFEZ

Al-Saddiq Al-Raddi was born in Sudan in 1969 and grew up in Omdurman, Khartoum. He started his career as a journalist and became the cultural editor of the Sudanese daily *Al-Ayyam* before moving to another daily *Al-Sudani*, where he was the head of its cultural section until he was forced into exile in 2012. His poetic talents were revealed at an early age when, in 1986 at the age of seventeen, he won the first prize in a major poetry competition; in the same year he became the youngest member elected to the Sudanese Writers' Union. In 1996, he published his first two collections, *Ghina' al-'Uzlah* (Songs of Solitude), and *Matahat al-Sultan* (The Sultan's Labyrinth) at once, revealing a body of work which immediately established him as both a distinguished new voice and as one of the formidable poets of his generation. His third collection, *Aqasi Shashat al-Isgha'* (*The Limits of the Screen of Listening*), appeared in 2000 and his *Collected Poems* was published in 2010.

Al-Saddiq's advent onto the literary scene was part of a changing literary sensibility in Sudan in the 1990s which was a result of the restrictions and repression following the coup of the Islamist, Omar al-Bashir, in 1989. Al-Saddiq belongs to a new generation of Sudanese writers whose cultural formation took place in the vacuum created by the exodus of most Sudanese intellectuals in the 1970s and 1980s who had been forced into exile as a result of increasingly harsh political and social pressures. As a result, his poetry is afflicted by a sense of orphanage, having little or no connection to dominant tradition that prevailed in Sudan before these upheavals. This was later heightened, in Al-Saddiq's case, by his abandonment of traditional poetic metre with its lyricism and soothing musicality, when he chose to write what is known as 'prose poetry' in Arabic, which is analogous to free verse in English. The 1990s were the heydays of the prose poem in Arabic literature, which constituted a poetic rupture with the past; the new Sudanese poets, bewildered by the disastrous death of grand narratives, embraced its aesthetics of quiet contemplative reflections that were clearly suited to a world wallowing in defeat, crises and corruption.

Gone were the days of lyricism and hope, of collective vision and optimism, of oratory and joyous musicality, and the new poet was busy finding the diction and form to suit his *Songs of Solitude*. He found guidance and solace in the poetry of the Sudanese, Muhammad Abdul-Hayy (1944–89), who died prematurely but is widely considered the father figure of Al-Saddiq's generation. Abdul-Hayy's poetry displayed a clear aversion to the hackneyed expressions and sonorous musicality that had dominated Sudanese poetry for generations. He shunned the predominance of ideological concerns, instead developing a keen interest in complex imagery, multilayered metaphors, mythic allusions, succinct diction, terse and well-structured poems, all the while keenly aware of the contradictions inherent in his position as an African poet writing in Arabic. These are also the types of poems that Al-Saddiq writes, for he once said that he attempts 'To radically change poetic language by enabling it to become multilayered, concerned as much with poetic structure as with thought, culture and metaphysics'. The metaphysical dimension of his poems is what distinguishes them from those of his contemporaries, and it is this multilayered structure that makes him so difficult to translate. Al-Saddiq also said, 'If the poem ceases to be multilayered, with a complex and sophisticated view of life, it ceases to be modern.'

The harsh climate and ruthless everyday reality of Sudan, with its cruel poverty and closed horizons, is balanced by and juxtaposed with its rich spirituality and fecund tradition of fantastic and mythical literature, which almost has a concrete presence in daily life. The poet captures these contradictions and renders them in poems like 'Lamps', 'Everything' and 'Theatre', poems which employ the binary of the beloved / homeland and transform it into an existential stance.

In 2005 he participated in the Poetry Translation Centre's first World Poets' Tour, and this encounter with another culture sharpened his poetic desire for a new type of poetry which manifests itself in 'Small Fox', 'Garden Statues' and 'In the Company of Michelangelo' with their suppressed internal yearning. They open a new way forward in his poetry, and are a testimony of the valuable impact of the work of the PTC on the world of poetry. The 'drowning man foundering in the treacherous waters' of 'Everything' and the lamps that 'are extinguished in the far-flung houses' of 'Lamps' are now being freshly cast in the bronze of that experience in 'Garden Statues'.

Al-Saddiq Al-Raddi: 'The Promise of Poetry'

SARAH MAGUIRE

Al-Saddiq Al-Raddi is widely regarded as one of the leading African poets writing in Arabic. And, although the Arabic of his poetry is stringently classical, he always writes from the position of being an African citizen of Sudan. His country has an extensive, complex history thanks to the extraordinary diversity of its people: more than two hundred languages are spoken there. Sudan has long been the crossing point of many major ancient trade routes (several still in active use today), both from eastern Africa to the country's western coast and from southern sub-Saharan Africa to the Mediterranean. Saddiq has an inexhaustible knowledge of the peoples and languages of his vast country and, unlike most Sudanese, he has travelled the length and breadth of what once was northern Sudan (South Sudan seceded in 2011). He is steeped in Sudanese music and art and alive to the cultures of nearby countries, such as Mali and Mauritania, which are inextricably connected with his own.

Saddiq is famous among the Sudanese not only because of his avowedly political poetry (not translated here since the density of its contextual references makes it all but impenetrable to outsiders) but because his lyric poems express a yearning for transcendence that speaks to his community. Perhaps the clearest example of this can be found in the final stanza of Saddiq's remarkable poem 'A Body' when, in response to the question, 'What is there?', he writes:

A body transcending my body.
A body exiled by desire.
A body sheltered by the wind.

This questioning of the nature of the self – its shifting identities, its permeable boundaries – is imbued with the mystical traditions of Sufi poetry. Sufism has a particularly strong presence in Sudan. Until forced into exile in 2012, Saddiq was born and lived all his life in Omdurman, one of the three cities that form greater Khartoum. Omdurman, famous for its richly diverse culture, sprang from the routed army of the Mahdi, the Sufi leader responsible for one of the most humiliating defeats in British military history when he vanquished 'Gordon of Khartoum' in 1885.[1]

Sudanese culture, with its love of music, poetry, dance and theatre, is infused with Sufism, the mystical tradition that is at the heart of Islam and which permeates the arts. It is a culture that celebrates desire and delight, a culture that is completely at odds with the repressive puritanism of the Saudi-backed, Wahhabi fundamentalist version of Islam.

In the West we tend to have a very simplistic idea of what 'political poetry' looks like, in effect generally confining it to the category of literal-minded 'protest poetry'. Strange as it may seem to those of us fortunate to have lived our lives in comfort and peace, articulating the right to joy is a potent threat to totalitarianism. It is hard for us to grasp the sheer audacity – and courage – of Saddiq's continuing to write poetry that expresses desire with such extraordinary frankness, while living in a regime that cleaves to the ideology of Islamic fundamentalism.

1 Nowadays, Sufism, famous for its celebration of music and poetry, is the 'acceptable' face of Islam in the West, held up as a peaceful alternative to Islamic fundamentalism. But it's worth remembering that, once upon a time, the Sufis, not the Wahhabis, were the West's Islamic bugaboos.)

The fantasies of 'purity' that are the bedrock of fascist thinking are inimical to difference, and in this, al-Bashir is no exception. His rule has been marked by a determination to turn Sudan into a monotheist, monocultural Islamicist society with Arabic the country's one accepted language and Arabism its objective. Shortly after he came to power in 1989, he banned the Writers' Union, shut down libraries and had all the books they housed destroyed – other than textbooks on maths, Arabic and Islam.

Saddiq's exquisite lyric poem, 'A Star', challenges the regime's repression on two fronts. Firstly, the poem speaks openly of a longing for transcendence – and then it unflinchingly confronts the mechanisms of oppression:

> In the green pits of our being our inner
> threads yearn; this radiance, that makes me feel I own
> herds of horses, am as inspired as any knight –
>
> what is its source? Shocked
> into words, I defied the book-burners, the suffocators
> of thought and feeling, all who'd censor and shroud knowledge.
>
> And a violet blossomed fiercely in the bosom of the sky.

Saddiq's most famous work, 'Poem of the Nile', is an outstanding example of his complex, multi-layered poetry. Written at the time of al-Bashir's 1989 coup, the poem describes the broken city of Khartoum with a dreamlike, post-apocalyptic intensity. Throughout, lines of description ('Poverty invades the children's playgrounds, leaving // Them silent, accursed, their heritage / Only anger and disbelief.') are interspersed with passages of heightened imagery:

And my soul would embark on a holy journey too,
For the silence suspended between us
Is a language floating among the ruins of a
beautiful, vanished past.

The breadth of reference in Saddiq's poetry subverts the 'purity' of the official tongue of Sudan's Islamist regime by referencing the multiracial plurality of his country's heritage. In particular, Saddiq is fascinated by Sudan's history of proud, ancient (pre-Islamic) kingdoms, a vision that directly challenges the ideological stranglehold of Sudan's dictatorship. For Saddiq, Sudan today is inseparable from its complex – often magnificent, often violent – history. Towards the end of 'Poem of the Nile' he remembers the ancient Nubian kingdom of Kush, its magnificent capital Meroe and King Piankhy, who ruled over Egypt:

And, see, the city of Meroe appears
And the face of the Nubian lover
Who walks among the sorrows of the waterwheels
Searching for warriors among the horses.
Where does the line of ancestral blood begin
And when does the blood loss reach its climax,
O King Piankhy, enthroned ruler of Kush,
A kingdom unravelling in bitter silence?[2]

By the time I founded the Poetry Translation Centre (PTC) in 2004, I had nearly a decade's experience of co-translating Arabic, mainly Palestinian, poetry. Thanks to personal friendships, I'd also developed

2 The Kingdom of Kush (1070 BCE to 350 CE) is one of the earliest and most impressive ancient states found south of the Sahara. Its ruined capital Meroe (800 BCE – 350 CE) is situated 200km north-east of Khartoum. Kushite emperors ruled as pharaohs of the twenty-fifth dynasty of Egypt for a century.

a long-standing interest in Sudan, and I was aware how little Sudanese poetry written in Arabic had been translated into English. In 2002, I inaugurated a series of poetry translation workshops when I was writer in residence at the School of Oriental and African Studies. I was delighted when the Sudanese writer and translator Hafiz Kheir introduced us to Saddiq's astonishing poetry. Later, when I established the PTC, I commissioned Hafiz to co-translate Saddiq with the British poet, Mark Ford. Saddiq was one of six international poets we invited o the UK to take part in the PTC's first World Poets' Tour in 2005. His wonderful poetry quickly gained him an appreciative audience among non-Arabic speakers. In addition, his arrival here was greeted with huge enthusiasm by the UK Sudanese community, who profoundly admired him for his outstanding poetry, and for his principled opposition to al-Bashir's dictatorship.

During the 2005 tour, the PTC was contacted by Professor Stephen Quirke, Curator of the Petrie Museum of Egyptian Archaeology at the University of London. The museum holds a significant collection of items from ancient Sudan, mainly from Meroe; but these – as the very name of the museum makes clear – tend to be obscured by the Petrie's Egyptian artefacts. Stephen was delighted to hear we had invited such an important Sudanese poet to the UK, and he was eager to work with us to find ways of encouraging the Sudanese community to view the relics of their country's fascinating history. As a result, during Saddiq's subsequent visits to the UK, we arranged a series of events – and some excellent parties – in the museum. This led to Saddiq being the appointed as the Petrie's poet in residence in 2012, commissioned to write a series of poems in response to the museum's Sudanese collections. Five of these commissioned poems are included here.[3]

3 The collection, *He Tells Tales of Meroe: Poems for the Petrie Museum,* which includes background information on the Petrie's collections and photographs of the objects that inspired Saddiq's poems, is available to purchase from the PTC. The poems and photographs also appear on our website.

One of the most impressive aspects of Saddiq's poetry is its range. In this volume you will find many of his exquisite, imaginative love poems ('Throne', 'A Star', 'Small Fox'); poems that consider Sudanese history ('Poem of the Nile', 'He Tells Tales of Meroe', 'Traces of an Unknown Woman'); and poems that examine writing and the difficulty and necessity of becoming a poet ('Theatre', 'Writing', 'Prayer'). In the astonishing sequence 'Weaving a World', desire, history and poetry come together – all three subjects can be found juxtaposed in the poem's seven sections.

The first poem of Saddiq's we translated in 2002 is the title poem of this collection. 'A Monkey at the Window' is both a remarkably delicate self-portrait of the poet as a child and a tender love poem to his 'wounded' mother. It is one of the most touching and heartfelt poems ever written by a son to his mother. The poem makes clear that it's their loving relationship that makes his poetry possible. She is the one who encourages him in his games of 'throwing little words and circles / out of the window'. And when she smiles, 'the whole world lights up':

> Once he made necklaces from seashells
> colouring them with his own fairytales
> once he made friends with strange frogs
> – and all the while she's watching him

But the poem is also imbued with a sense of loss. He describes how his mother is lured away by songs, by 'tender fingers / and her own translucent solitude'. And home itself is far from being a haven, with its 'woodworms / gnawing through your heart' and the 'hammering of enemies and relatives'. What saves him is his 'sole secret': 'the creak of the universe' and the belief that 'you are / the key'. What saves him is the promise of poetry – the poems you now hold in your hands.

A MONKEY AT THE WINDOW

قردٌ على الشباك

قصائد مختارة

قردٌ على الشبّاك

1

الولدُ الذي كان يلهو في السرير

أمّه تطبخُ بجروحةً

يرمي بالدوائرِ واللغوِ

من النافذة الصغيرةْ

تبتسمُ

(يسطع العالمُ كلّه)

"يُبَرْطِمُ" — ماذا يظنُّ ؟!

على الشبّاك قردٌ

وراء البابْ

لكنه لم يزلْ يهوي إلى ظلمةٍ بعيدةٍ

لا يدلِّي صراخاً

يعلِّي مخالبَهُ – الولدُ

الأخضرُ

المُستَفَزُّ

2

لم تعلّمه البكاءَ —بغتةً — الغناءْ

خضراءُ — كما شاءت

تعلّمه الأقاصي والشسوعْ

وتناديه: الرحابةْ

خلفه تلٌّ من الوصفِ

أمامه نهرٌ وجرعةُ ليلٍ

قوافلُ تدعوه لينأى

(أين هذا الخيطُ

A Monkey at the Window

1

The little boy, playing in bed
while his wounded mother cooks,
is throwing little words and circles
out of the window.

> She smiles
> (the whole world lights up)
> he chatters excitedly – What can he see?

There's a monkey at the window –
behind the door!
    But he is falling
        into darkness.
            And though he never raises a cry
he holds up his claws – this dark
      stormy
         boy.

2

She never taught him how to cry, only how to sing.
Happy in herself – just as she wished to be –
she taught him endless space and vastness
and she calls him: open-hearted.

Behind him a mountain of metaphors
in front, a river, a mouthful of night
and a train of caravans calling him away.
(Where is that thread

تلك النارُ

أين الملكاتْ؟!)

3

راكضاً في زقاقٍ

يدلقُ الزيتَ

على السروالِ — هذا الولدْ !

بالَ على السروالِ

من أثرِ الضحك

وهو يركضُ في الأبدْ

هذا الزقاقُ

عصابةُ الجراءِ

تواطؤُ الغيوبْ

4

البابُ مصنوعٌ — يوحي بيدٍ تعرَقُ

المفتاحُ أنتَ

صريرُ الكون — سِرُّكَ

الوحيدْ

تسندُ عليه قفا مستقبلٍ وترائيات

وتحملُ عنه أكولةَ "الأَرْضَةِ"

في قلبِكَ

رائحةُ البَلَلِ

مطارقَ الأعداءِ والأقاربْ

(طالت غيبةُ الضوءِ

يدهنُ الأشياءَ بالصحوِ

طالَ حضورُ الطلاءْ)

that fire
the skill?)

3
Running – down an alleyway
he splashes cooking oil all down his shorts this boy!

He wets himself
with laughter
running through Eternity –
      through this alleyway
      this pack of dogs
      the conspiracies of fate!

4
The solid front door remembers
the hand that made it –
      You are
          the key –
and the creak of the universe –
it's your sole secret.
You lean your future and your dreams against it.
For its sake you endure the woodworms
gnawing through your heart
the reek of damp
the hammering of enemies and relatives.
(Long is the absence of light
      that paints things awake –
      Long is the presence of paint!)

You come home exhausted – from wherever you've been
the wind at your side – just as you wished –
toyed with by traumas.

تدخلُ – منْ أيِّ شئتَ – مثقوبَ العناءِ

تصاحبكَ الريحُ – شئتَ

تداعبكَ الصدماتُ !

كانَ ينظمُ عقداً من الأصدافِ

يلوّنه بخرافاته

ويصادقُ الضفادعَ الغريبةْ

وهي ترقبه بصمتٍ

وراء الباب / على الشبّاكِ

(تُهْرَعُ كي تُعلّي

لايُدلّي

أيَّ شَيْءٍ)!

5

بالغابةِ   ألوحيدةُ تعرفُ الأصواتْ

كانت تناديها عيونُ الغالين

تشدُّها أناشيدُهُم

بحنانِ أناملهم

ورهيفِ توحُّدها

تقعُدُ صامتةً

قُربَ أيَّ شَيْءٍ

تدفِّئُ الشايَ

أو تصنعُ العصيدةْ

في الحديقة

بالبيت الغريبِ – بيتها

تدعو مواعينَ الغسيلِ

إلى صباح الصوت

تدلكُ كلَّ شَيْءٍ في مكانه

22

Once he made necklaces from seashells
and colouring them with his own fairy tales
once he made friends with strange frogs
– and all the while she's watching him
from behind the door / from out the window
(when she runs to pick him up
  he will not raise
  a cry!)

5
In the forest the lonely one knows all the voices
beckoned by the eyes of loved ones
their songs are luring her
with their tender fingers
and her own translucent solitude.
  She sits in silence
  close to every thing
  brewing tea
  stirring the porridge.

In the garden
of a strange home, her home
she welcomes pots and pans
to the sounds of morning.
  Scrubbing everything in its proper place
  one eye on the radio
  that calls her to those distant sands
  the desert.

تراقبُ المذياع

يدعوها إلى رملٍ بعيد

صحراءَ

لكن لونُها يمتدُّ نهراً

...كي يغنِّي

والوَلَدْ ؟!

... ...

في غابةٍ خضراءَ

...أو حمراءَ

في صحراءَ

من كان يناديها — أبَدْ ؟!

But her colours flow like a river
so she can sing…
                    And that boy?
…   …   …
In a green forest
or a red forest
or a desert
now who calls him to Eternity?

Translated by Sarah Maguire and Hafiz Kheir

جسد

جُثّةُ طائرٍ بِفَمِكَ
تَبْعَثُ الأُغْنية.
نَيّئاً
من عيونِكَ ينطلِقُ الضّوءُ
في عُرْيِهِ الكامِل

عليكَ أنْ تُرْسِلَ الأُفْقَ، مَرّةً كي تُفيقَ، عليكَ
أنْ تبعثَ نافذةً تِلْوَ أُخرى
تَسْنِدُ الجِّدارْ

أتْرُكُ الأبجديةَ تتعلّقُ بي
وأنا أتسلّقُ خيطَ اللُّغةِ الرّفيع
بيني والعالَم.
أتَجَمْهَرُ في فَمي
معلّقاً بين اللُّغةِ والعالَم
بين العالَم والأبجديةٌ.

أتركُ رأسي
يُنْصِتُ
للخرافةِ
أُصغي لمديحِ الجِّهاتِ لبعضِها
وأزمْجِرُ للرّيحِ من قُوّةِ الجَبَل

ما لساني يقولُ ليَ أصْعِدِ المسافةَ
ما المسافةُ بين صوتي وحنيني
ما هناكْ
!؟

26

A Body

The body of a bird in your mouth
breathing songs.
Raw light spills from your eyes,
utterly naked.

You must breach the horizon, once,
in order to wake up.
You must open window after window.
You must support the walls.

I let alphabets cling to me
as I climb the thread of language
between myself and the world.
I muster crowds in my mouth:
suspended between language and the world,
between the world and the alphabets.

I let my head
listen to the myth,
to all sides praising each other.
And I shout at the winds from the top of a mountain.

Why does my tongue tell me to climb this far?
What is the distance between my voice and my longing?
What is there?

جَسَدٌ يترفَّعُ عن جسدي

جسدٌ تَنْفِيهِ الرَّغبة

جسدٌ تَعْلُوهُ الرِّيح.

A body transcending my body.
A body exiled by desire.
A body sheltered by the wind.

Translated by Sarah Maguire and Atef Alshaer

كلُّ شَيْءٍ

إطلق الرِّيحَ من فَمِ الصيَّادِ
إلى هيكلِ المَرْكَبِ ، من عُمْقِ الشراعِ
وفَكِّكِ الرُّبَطِ عن فَمِ النهرِ
أُصرخْ
أيها الغريقُ
في اللُّجَجِ الدائرةْ

يبدأُ النهرُ من عاداته، ساكناً
يبدأُ الشاطئُ لَمَّ الشموسِ
من أفواهِ السمكِ المَيِّتِ
يبدأُ طَهْوِ الظلالِ
من الرائحةِ، كنسَ الحصى

لكنَّ الهدوء – الريح – أصوات
الذين يركبون المقالع – لكنَّ السكونْ

يبحرونَ من ليلٍ بعيدٍ
يحفرونَ الماءَ بالصبر العتيدِ
وينظرونَ العَتْمَةَ

بينما أبَحرتَ قُربَ الصباحِ
من محاياتِ التي في صدرِهَا
أَثبَّ مَعنى
قادماً منها وتطلبُ الضفةَ – خضرةَ العمرِ وأوراق الهويةِ
بينما أخرى تؤجِّركَ البسيطةَ
بين عينيها
وتطلبُ صفوَ أوراقِ الكتابةِ – كلَّ شَيْءٍ !

30

Everything

Let the wind blow from a fisherman's mouth,
from the span of a sail to the shell of a boat,
unlocking the mouth of the river –
So, shout, drowning man, when you founder
in treacherous waters

At dawn, the river embarks in silence
Riverbanks glean suns from the scales of dead fish
Jostled by eddies, the aroma of flotsam and jetsam
bakes in the shade

Becalmed, a breeze freights the stillness
Sails lazily unfurl

They sail all night from afar,
ploughing the river with ritual persistence,
staring darkness straight in the eye

You set sail at dawn,
infused with the tincture of a heart
that had beached your whole life ashore

And yet, another beloved
is offering you heaven on earth in her glance,
demanding only the perfection of poetry – everything!

Translated by Sarah Maguire and Sabry Hafez

لا شَيْءْ

قبل أَنْ تَشْرَعَ في القِرَاءَةِ
ضَعْ القَلَمْ
وَانْظُرْ إلى الحِبْرِ السَائِلِ
كَمْ يَفْهَمُ في النَزْفِ.

تَفَقَّهْ

في مِسَاحَةِ الأُفُقِ
وضِيقِ البَصَرِ، إِتِّسَاعِ البَصِيرَةِ
وَخُذْلانِ الأَصَابِعْ

ولا تَلُمْني/ لا تَلُمْ أَحَداً
إنْ مِتُّ قبل أَنْ تَقْرأَ لا شَيْءَ
قبل أَنْ نَفْهَمَ في النَزْفِ!

32

Nothing

Before you start reading,
put down your pen:
consider the ink,
how it comprehends bleeding

Learn
from the distant horizon
and from narrowing eyes
the expansiveness of vision
and the treachery of hands

Do not blame me – do not blame anyone –
if you die before you read on
before blood is understood

Translated by Sarah Maguire and Atef Alshaer

مسرح

1

كلُّ هذه الحروبْ
ليصبحَ العالمُ مُوحِشاً
من أجل أن يصدأ البيتُ
كي تنام
موجَّعاً بالكارثةْ
كلُّ هذا الحبّ
من أجل أن تنطقَ العظامُ بـ لا أحدْ
كلُّ هذا الموتْ
لأجل أن نلتقي
فقطْ !؟

2

أُكتبْ
فَلْيَشْتَغِلِ العالمُ فيك
من بين يديكَ
ولْتَشْتَعِلْ بالبذاءةِ روحُ الجسدْ
فيكَ ما يَمْحُو ويُمْحَى
داءُ الحِبْرِ
عَرَقُ الشُّغْلِ واللّهاثِ
من بيتٍ وصالةٍ
لشارعٍ وعراءْ

أُكتبْ
بمشيئةِ العارفِ
بكلٍّ ما بين يديك
من قصبٍ وخيوطْ

34

Theatre

1

All these wars
make the world unhomely
make homes rust apart
make you fall asleep, riddled with calamities

All this love
yet loneliness still cuts you to the bone

All this death
just so we can meet –
nothing more?

2

Write
to set the world ablaze
so poetry quickens in your hands
and inflames you with desire

Write, and wipe the slate
Infected by writing
you sweat in agony
from a bedsit
to the street and out into the wild

Write
in full knowledge
of everything that's in your hands
both quill and string at your disposal

بخبرة الرائي، ما يحرِّكُ الجسدَ
يفيدُ الفضاءُ

3

هذا العالَمُ الصغيرُ — أمامَكَ
المصنوعُ من القشِّ والدُّبَارَة والمَلَلْ
الذي يتسرَّبُ من بين الأصابعِ كالأحلامِ
تَذْرُوه الروحُ
وتمتصَّه — أنتَ — كالرائحةْ

هل تخافُ الحشراتِ — تحتمي فيه من النورِ كلّه
أم تخافُ الدَمَ — تَعَافُ براءَةَ السيِّدِ فيه
تختشي من الأصابعِ والخِفَّةِ والشموعْ ؟!

هذا العالَمُ المفتوحُ أمامكَ
يُغنيكَ عن السؤالِ
هل يُسَاوِي ثمنَ الحبرِ الذي كُتِبَ به
ثمنُ الدمعِ — بعدُ — لم يَجَفْ؟!

4

معقوفٌ — زمنُ النورِ — تحسّه يلسعُ صفحةَ الوجهِ
تحسّه هي
وهي تمسحُ — الخوانَ — حائلَ اللّونِ
خلفَ السريرِ
لكنه بغتةً كالخنجرِ
يدخلُ قلبَ الظُلْمَةِ
يُبْحِرُ ببهاءِ العالمِ كلّه
بطينِ العناقِ وعتمةِ التعرّفِ بالبَلَلْ
يتركُ الوجهَ مُرتبكاً

36

Write
certain of what electrifies the body
sure of how to rig the scene

3
This little world beneath you
made of boredom, balsawood and string
jerks between your fingers in a dream
Spirited away
you drink it in like scent

Are you scared of scorpions? Are you scared of blood?
Take refuge in the wings
But beware the spotlights, beware of being fingered

This little world beneath you
is here to give you all the answers
Is it worth the precious ink that wrote it –
the cost of these fresh tears?

4
Light stings the page of your face
And it strikes her
as she dusts the faded wardrobe near the bed –
like a dagger, suddenly
it rends the dark
blazing with the whole world's brilliance,
leaves her flushed,
spoored, wet
and flat out in astonishment

يتركُها بِأُضْطِجَاعةِ الذهولْ !

5

واحدٌ، الأبيضُ
واحدةٌ، الجهاتُ
كلُنا نتشبَّثُ بالحيرةِ والحبرِ والرحيلْ

نَسكنُ أحلامَنا وننشرُ المناديلَ
نُبشِّرُ الحاناتِ بالمرايا والغثيانْ
بدوائرِ الدخانِ والحكايا
من كلِّ أبيضَ نعدِّدُ الحبرَ
يتحدُ الدمعُ
تنبثقُ الدهشةُ
من كلِّ جهةٍ تسطعُ القبورْ !

6

أراكَ مُنتظراً باباً وراءَكَ
يُفْتَحُ بالرَّبَّابةِ
كي تَدْخُلَ الماضي بمستقبلٍ لا يُشِينْ

مضيئاً قواربكَ التي تحطَّمتْ من الرُّسُوِّ
مُقْعِداً أقاصيكَ الرحيبة
مثلَ دَانٍ
طائراً تمتحنُ السجيَّةَ

والذين من أمامكَ في السَّهْوِ
يَعْتَمِرونَ، تمرُّ فوانيسُهم عبرَ بابِكَ
مُسْوَدَّةٌ صحائفُ الفجرِ
من أثرِ الغروبْ

5

We latch on to bewilderment, to ink, and to departure
Living in our dreams, unfurling handkerchiefs,
we bring news to the bars of mirrors and nausea,
smoke-rings, gossip, tales
From the oneness of white we plumb our ink,
from the oneness of all directions
Tears merge
Surprise arrives
All around you tombstones rise

6

Waiting in front of a door that's behind you,
I watch it open with a rabab
so you can go back to the past with your spotless future,
refilling your boats with light after they'd rotted through ashore,
restocking the wares of your mighty stories
like a bird refurbishing its nest

Those who went before you
live in a stupor,
their lanterns barging through your door
The flush of dawn
blackened
by the taint of dusk
Your face is familiar,

كانَ وَجهُكَ يُعْرَفُ

والبابُ خلفَكَ

وجَهُ الذي من أمامكَ

كيفْ ؟!

.... تدخلُ الماضي بمستقبلٍ لا يشينْ !

7

هذا ثمنُ الحربِ: ولاؤكَ الدائمُ

لكفاءةِ التهريجِ

تِكْنيكِ البراءةُ

هذا ثمنُ الحبِّ: عقوقُكَ الدائمُ لأُبُوَّةِ التَّكْنيكِ

أُمومَةِ الكفاءةُ

هذا ثمنُ الموتِ: بقاؤكَ الدائمُ حيّاً

بقبرِ الحبِّ وساحةِ الحربِ

بقاؤكَ الدائمُ في هُوَّةِ الطَّاعةِ

في مَسْقَطِ العالمْ !.

but what about the face in front of you
faced towards the door behind you?
...   ... as you go back to the past with your blameless future

7
The price of war: perpetual loyalty;
eschewing tomfoolery;
feigning naivety

The price of love: ceaseless quarrels
with the fathers of procedures
and the mothers of proficiency

The price of death: eternal life
in the grave of love and the theatre of war
Life at the ends of obedience
Life at the end of the world

Translated by Sarah Maguire and Sabry Hafez

ورقة

يا مَلِكَ الْمُنَافَاتِ الْبَعِيدَةْ
مَنْ رَآكَ
يا صَدِيقَ الشَّهْقَةِ والصَّمْتْ

مَنْ أَبْصَرَ الشَّارِعَ في دَمِكْ
مَنْ هَيَّأَ للسَاعَةِ
زَفَافَ الصَّرْخَةِ
هَيَّأَ للقُضْبَانِ حِدَادَ الْجُدْرِ
وَمُوتُ العَالَمِ في كَلِمَةْ؟!

تَسْقُطُ   ذَاكِرَةُ المُدْنِ الْعَطِنَةْ
تَسْقُطُ   أَحْلَامُ العَالَمْ
يَسْقُطُ   تَارِيخُ الأَمْسَاخْ

Record

King of the distant cries
Companion of screaming and silence –
Who saw you?

Who saw the blood on your roads?
Who prepared the watch and the spectacle of fear?
Who built the walls and threw a guard around them?
Who made the world die in the space of a word?

Memories of cities – fall
Expectations – fall
Histories of forgery – fall

Translated by Sarah Maguire and Atef Alshaer

يظنونني ملكاً وأنا الملك

حاجتي للكلمةْ
حاجةُ السَّابقِ للحَجَرِ والنَّارِ
حاجتُه للبَلْطةِ والرُّمْحِ والدرعِ
للأُنْسِ بالنايِّ..

أثريتُكِ
أثريتُ ظنَّ الحياةِ بأيّامِها والذئبَ بلياليه
أثريتُ جوعَ الفرادةِ
بقيتُ لا للموعظةِ أو ثمن الفراءِ
بقيتُ فأبقيتُ كَسْبَ السبيَّة حيّاً
..
ما أكلتهُ الحروبُ بقاياكَ
ما ألهمَ المُهْمَلَ
واحدٌ من رعايا فتنتكِ المُفترِسَة!
فطنتني
أخذتني بعيداً بجهلي
يظنونني ملكاً وأنا المَلِكْ.

They Think I Am a King: Yes, I Am the King

I need the Word
like my ancestor's need for stone and fire
like his need for an axe, for a spear, for a shield
like his need for the solace of a flute . . .

I enriched you
like life is enriched by day
like a wolf is enriched by a night with no moon
I enriched the longing for transcendence
I stayed neither to preach nor to barter with the skins of animals
I stayed to bear witness to the dignity of women enslaved
. .
Wars consumed your remains
Their traces captivated your disciples
in thrall to your fierce charm
You taught me
You delivered me from ignorance
They think I am a king:
Yes, I am the King

Translated by Sarah Maguire and Rashid El Sheikh

This poem was written during Al-Saddiq al-Raddi's residency at the Petrie Museum of Egyptology. It was inspired by the painted sandstone figure of a flute player, from the royal ritual bath at Meroe. The museum holds a significant collection of items from the ancient city of Meroe which was the capital city of the Kingdom of Kush from c.800 BCE to c.350 CE.

قيلولة الآلهة

ثَمَّةَ الحَجَرُ المَلِكُ
المَلِكةُ الحَصاةُ

قادةُ الجُنْدِ يفعلون الحربَ
صُكَّتْ النّقودُ– وقتها– حُلْيَةً
لِجرارِ وَقْتٍ مُملِ
وقتٌ أظمأُ للدَم
تَنْقدُهُ رؤوسَ متطايرةً: مَلِكاً
إثْرَ مَلِكٍ
وقتٌ تنقدُهُ سبيكةَ الوقتْ

لتكتملَ اللعبةَ: لابُدَّ من حُفْرةٍ خاليةْ
لابُدَّ مِنْ حَصاةٍ وحَجَرْ
لابُدَّ مِنْ أضحيةٍ وقربانْ
نصيبُكَ حفرةٌ خاليةْ
مَهْرُكِ سِرٌّ كشفتهُ الكِنايةْ

أخيراً؛ ثمة حجرٍ يحنُّ إلى كهفه
ثَمَّ حَصاةٍ تحنُّ إلى شاطيء النّهْر
أخيراً جَرّةٌ مُفْتقدةٌ– مطمورةٌ السِّرِّ؟!
ليست تلك هي المعضلة:
ثمة ملكٍ معطوبٍ ثمة تاجٍ يُتوَّجُ للهاويّة!

46

Killing Time

Here a stone is King,
the Queen, a pebble.

When there's time to kill,
coins become trinkets
hoarded in vases
and commanders make war.
Killing time
by scattering the heads
of one king after the next,
they fall for ingots of time.

When the final hole is taken
by stone or pebble –
by a sacrifice or an offering –
then the game is up.
Your lot
is that vacant hole.
Your dowry,
the mystery of a metaphor.

In the end there is a stone, aching for its cave,
a pebble, longing for the riverbank.
In the end, an abandoned earthenware pot –
repository of enigmas.
But that's just a game –
reality is a crippled king
and a crown that straddles the abyss.

Translated by Sarah Maguire and Rashid El Sheikh

*Written during Al-Saddiq al-Raddi's residency at the Petrie Museum in response to
a sandstone slab with six hemispheres carved into the rock, grouped round a seventh
hole in the centre. Now in the museum's collection of items from Meroe, the slab
was probably used as a board-game or for rituals of divination (500 BCE to 100 CE).*

العالَمُ – نَسيجُ الأصابع

صُورَةٌ

خَارِجٌ من كِهوفٍ بذَاكِرَتي للفضاءْ
بعصافيرَ مَيِّةٍ عَبْرَ ثُقْبِ الظلامِ الوحيدْ
بِمَعَادِنَ شَكَّلْتُهَا بدَمِي شَجَراً
لا يُظِلُّ مرايا تماثيلِها
للهواءِ بِنَفْسي وأَجْنِحتي

مَنْ يُخَبِّئُ لي شَارعاً
حين أخطو وحيداً إلى وطني
حين أحملُ شمساً
وأمشي إلى جسدي في عراءِ الحريقْ؟!.

يُتْم

لأَنِّي وحيدٌ هنا بالعراءِ
ولا سِرَّ لي
منذ أكتوبرَ المُحْتَرَقْ
كانَ لابدَّ لي أَنْ أُفَتِّشَ عن قَمرٍ
أَنْ أواجهَ امرأةً
في الحقولِ البعيدةِ: عُرْياً لِعُرْيْ
أَنْ أُفَتِّشَ عن وطنٍ يَخْتَمي
مِنْ شِتَاءِ الغيابِ بوهجِ أصابِعِها
بالحليبِ المُقَدَّسِ من شَطْرِها
لأُخبِّئَ أبريلَ مِنْ دَمِهِ
في دَمِي

Weaving a World

An Image
From the dark spaces of memory
   I emerged, rising through a pinprick of light
   in the gloom, on all sides the falling
   bodies of dead song-birds: these trees
that cast no shadow on their own reflections – I
fashioned them, forging, hammering, working the metal.
   And so I found myself, in the wind, fully fledged ...
Who
will keep clear a road for me, care
about the solitary journey
I make, torch in hand, in search of home,
or stride towards this body when it's
   blackening in the blazing desert heat?

Lost
Out of reach, stripped bare, orphaned,
betrayed by the secret fires
that October ignited,
I set about searching, searching
   for a consoling guide like the moon: for a woman
   also stripped bare, in a distant field,
   whose fingers might cradle, whose body
   might shelter, whose breast
   might nurture this aching for home.

كانَ لابُدَّ لي
أنْ أقولَ وداعاً وسَهْلاً
لعرشِ السماءِ المُضيءْ
أنْ أفجِّرَ جُرْحاً بنسيانِهِ
ضِدَّ هذا الفضاءْ!

وقتٌ آخَر

كان لابُدَّ لي
أنْ أعرِّفَ نَفْسي بأشجَارِها
أنْ أزوِّجَ نَفْسي فُكَاهتها نَفْسَها
مِنْ مَخيطِ الهواءِ العميقْ
بالدُّمُوعِ التي لا تَخيطُ الكَفَنْ

كان لابُدَّ لي
أنْ أقولَ وأمضي إلى كَهْفِ رُوحي
غَريباً بفاكِهتي وأصَابِعها

لأنِّي أنا الضُّوءُ يلْبَسُ أجْنِحَةَ الأرْضِ
والجُرْحُ يَرْفُو دَمَ القَلْبِ

لأنِّي أنا الليْلُ وأسْمي فسيحٌ على الأمْكِنَةْ
النَّهَارُ الذي يتَّسِخْ
بالنَّهَارِ على خطوتي
أخْلَعُ اللَّيلَ عنه
وأمْشِي على الوقتِ مُتَّسعاً في طَريقي.

Further,
I had somehow to hide
the frail, blood-stained shoots of April
inside me; I had to allow the crimson night-sky
its majesty; I had
to learn how to stain
the space of the present
with what seeps from a forgotten wound.

Another Time
Feeling my way through an inner forest, I practised
the art of self-possession: at times my own jokes
had me laughing out loud.

From the dense air
that surrounded me I gathered
the tears that stitch no shroud.

I bequeath to strangers all
I had to say, and the touch of my loves; the cell
or cave of my retreat is the shape of my soul.

What am I there? The light that floats
or the wound that streams or the dark
itself? Can words name it? What am I there?
To walk through day and night, both in time, and on it …

نَسِيجُ الأَصابعِ

المعلَّقُ سَقفاً على صَمتِهِ وحنينِ سُلالاتِهِ
دَائماً يَشتَهِي دَمَهُ
تُربةً للغناءْ
دَائماً يَشتَهِي
مَنْ يَقُودُ أَصَابِعَهْ
مَنْ يَكُونُ الطِّيورَ التي لا تُغَنِّي جَنازَتَهُ
كأنَّ الذي لا يَمُوتُ وحيداً
هو الكَائنُ الخيطُ
يَخْلَعُ مسمارَهُ عن نَسيجِ الجِّدَارِ
كأنَّ الذي لا يَكُونُ وحيداً
هو الكَائنُ العنكبوتْ

إضاءة

كيفَ كُنتِ تقودينَ لي قَمراً
حين أُطْفِئُ دَمعَكِ بين الأَصابعِ
بين الأَصابعِ حين أُضيءُ حنينَكِ
حين تَقُودينَ لي خنجراً
كيف كنتِ هنا وهناكْ
كيف كُنَّا مَعاً؟!.

حنين

حين كنتُ خليعاً بِنَفسِي
بلا هَمِّ قُوتْ
وأنا أَشتهي سِرَّكِ الملْتَبِس
وَرَقُ التُوتْ - نَفْسُهُ - لم يكن نَفْسَهُ
كيف أَلْبَسُهُ
في الحنينِ الغَريبِ إلى كائنٍ لا يموتْ؟!

Weaving

Swaying beneath the ceiling, silent, brooding
on ancestors, all the time longing
         to hear
         his blood sing –
or for someone to take and guide
his fingers, and sing songs that refute dying …
he likes to think that those who spin
and weave won't die alone. Slowly
he removes a leg from the wall.
Others may live alone, but not spiders as patient,
as industrious as he is.

Close Up

How beautifully you offered
me the moon, as I caressed
away your tears, and you, alight
with love, thrust
at my vitals with a kitchen knife.
Was I here   or there?
How one we were!

Longing

I got undressed.
I was beyond hunger, obsessed
with the mystery of you.
How, why should I
conceal my longing with senseless
fig-leaves? While I
was naked, you were immortal.

حلم

وَلْتَكُنْ جَسَداً أَخْضَرَ يا أَيُّها الشِّعْرُ
كُنْ لُغَةً أَتَغَرَّبُ فيها بِنَفْسي وأَجْنِحَتي
نَفَساً في لِساني
لأَرْعَى قَبائِلَ صَوْتي – على صَمْتِها
ساهِراً ووحيداً أَرى

لم تَكُ جَسَداً أَخْضَرَ
لم تَكُ سَيِّداً طَيِّباً تُشْتَرى
لم تَكُ رَبَّةً
أَيُّها الهَذَيانُ الذي أَشْتَهي، يَتُها الذّاكِرَةْ!

هَيْكَلْ

لِمَ كنتِ معي جَسَداً ظَامِئاً في فِراشِي
وعَارِيَةً بالسَّماءِ
ومَسْقُوفَةً بالنُّجومْ؟!
لِمَ كنتِ المِياهَ الغَرِيقَةَ في جَسَدِي
حين كنتُ الغُيومْ
الغُيومُ التي كالحَمائِمِ تَطَّايَرُ الرُّوحُ مِنها
الغُيومُ التي أَرْتَوي نَوْمُها ساهِياً
في الشِّتاءِ البعيدِ عَرَقْ
لِمَ كنتِ سِهامَ الأَرَقْ
ضِدَّ قلبي
وكنتِ الرِّياحَ الصَّدِيقَةَ في جسدي
حين كنتُ الغيومْ!
لِمَ كنتِ الوحيدةَ عارِيةً تَحْتَ هَيْكَلِ كَيْنُونَتي
حيثُ أَقْبِضُ – حين أُرِيحُ السَّماءَ – طيورَ الأَبَدْ!.

Sacred

You were the thirsty body
next to mine in bed, the sky
your blanket and the constellations your roof: why?

You were the deep waters in my body
when, sweating through winter, I daydreamed I was a cloud
of rain, dove-white, aflutter with souls: why?

You were the barbs of insomnia
tearing my breast, and the friendly winds
coursing through me, driving these streaming rain-clouds: why?

You, naked, were the only one present and sacred
instant when, moving the sky to one side,
I reached out and caught hold of the birds of eternity: why?

Dream

Poem – may you be green
and alive, a world
through which I wander aloft
on wings, with my whole
being. Inspire my tongue
until the tribes that inhabit my voice,
long silent, are fed again.
Poem – alone and sleepless,
I find you are neither green
nor alive, nor a kind master
nor a muse-figure, but an addictive
fusion of delirium and memory!

Translated by Mark Ford and Hafiz Kheir

*April and October: References to two successful peaceful uprisings,
in October 1964 and April 1985, staged by the Sudanese people against
the military dictators, General Aboud (1958–64) and General Nimeiri
(1969–85), both of which introduced brief periods of democracy
(Sudan has been ruled by the dictator, Omar al-Bashir since 1989).*

نص

1

رَأَيْتُ المَلاكْ

والعَصَافِيرَ مَذْبُوحَةً
ورأيتُ الحصانْ
العَسَاكِرَ
والشَّجَرِ المَيِّتِ
السيِّدَاتِ الحَزِينَاتِ
السِّيِّدَاتِ الوَلُوفَاتِ عَلَى الوَلْوَلاتِ – الصُّراخْ

رَأَيْتُ الشوارعَ والعَرَبَاتِ الأنيقَاتِ مُسْرِعَةً
رأيتُ المَرَاكِبَ و"الشُّفَّعَ" الأَبْرِيَاءْ

قلتُ كيف هو الطِّينُ يا سيِّدي الماءْ
في هذه الحَالْ
كيف الدُّخَانُ – الظِّلالُ – الروائحُ
لكنَّني
لم أَقُلْ – عَامِداً – كيفَ حَالُ البيوتْ

Poem

I saw the angel
and the singing birds slaughtered.
I saw the horse,
the soldiers,
the grieving women,
the dead trees, and other women
inured to screams and wailing.
I saw the streets, the gusting wind,
the sports cars
racing by, the boats, the innocent kids.

I said, 'Master of the Water, this is
how things are: tell me about the clay,
the fire, the smoke, the shadows, the smell
of reality'. Deliberately, I did not ask
about our homes.

Translated by Mark Ford and Hafiz Kheir

مصابيح

في الماءِ
في صَمْتي وقُرْبِكِ
في نارٍ – وَحْدَهَا تجمَعُنا
أطفُو ..
ووحْدَكِ قد تُنَادِينَ عَلَيَّ!

....

يدخُلُ الطائرُ طقسَ الأخضرِ
مثلَ الوَتَر
بَرْقٌ يَرِفُّ على العينِ كالسِّرِّ
تنحني قُبْلَةٌ في القوسْ
يَسْتَمِرُّ المطر!

في الشوارعِ لم يَعُدْ أصدقائي
في البيوتِ البعيدةِ عن بعضِها
لم تَعُدِ المصابيحْ
في القلبِ عادتْ رَجَّةُ النَّبْضِ المبعثرِ
لكنَّكِ تَرْمِينَ المناديلَ على الرَّاحِلِ
والباقي على نورِ الصباح!

Lamps

In the water
in silence at your side
in a fire that draws us close
I drift –
and only you can call me

. . . .
A bird enters spring
like a lance
Your eyes flash their secrets
A kiss grazes the rainbow
The rain rains

But the streets are empty of my friends
Lamps are extinguished
in the far-flung houses
and the lost heart echoes in its lonely chamber

You give your blessings to those who depart
and leave the rest to fate

Translated by Sarah Maguire and Sabry Hafez

مَدارْ

وقتُكَ مُكَدَّسٌ ، أيّها الماضي
إلى عربةٍ أو طريقٍ
يبعثرُ اللهاتَ
يمزجُ الكأسَ بالخنجرْ

مُرْهَقٌ كي تكابدَ حلمكَ
في خطوةٍ هرئةٍ
بحصانٍ ورغبةٌ
غَريقٌ بكلِّكَ في الكَلَلِ
من كلِّ شَيْءٍ
وتبشِّرُ بالحرائقِ والهتافْ

وقتُكَ المطلَقُ ، أيّها الماضي
من الساحةِ والسجنِ
مفتوحٌ بمرارةٍ وظنونْ .

Trajectory

Time engulfs you: the past
piles up on a cart or in the street
It winds you
Your glass becomes a weapon

Enduring your dream
you hesitate
between a horse and desire
Plunged into lethargy
you wager fire in the streets

Absolute time: your past –
from the square to the prison
salted with bitterness and doubt

Translated by Sarah Maguire and Atef Alshaer

قصيدة النيل – قراءة الشمس

سورة:

تصعدُ الجدرانُ في اللبلاب
والخرطوم واقفةٌ
على ساقٍ تغنِّي
هل ينامُ النيلُ؟!
كُنَّا عاشقَيْنِ نهدهدُ الأطفالَ
– ما اسْمي؟!
– أُسَمِّيكِ حضورَ الأرضِ فاقتربي
– وما طعمُ البكاءِ؟!
– ... ...
إفترقنا!.

سورة:

النيلُ يمضي هادئاً
ينسابُ في صمتِ المدينةِ
واحتراقاتِ القرى
والأصدقاءُ الآن
لا يتبادلونَ تحيةَ الصُّبْحِ
ولا يتعارفونَ
وأنبياءُ الفَقْرِ في كُلِّ الأماكنِ
يرشفون الشَّايَ والحزنَ
ولا يتحدَّثونَ
يخبِّئُونَ الموتَ في أطرافِهِم
ويوزِّعونَ الصَّبْرَ للأطفال
ينتشرونَ في الأشجارِ عَبْرَ الأرضِ
ينتحرونَ في اللَّيلِ احتجاجاً

62

Poem of the Nile

Prelude:
Walls climb the ivy
And Khartoum, poised on its unamputated foot
      Singing
Will the Nile ever escape into sleep?
We were the most loving of lovers, children trickling from us
            –   What name do you give me?
            –   I call you Presence of Earth
            –   Come closer then
            –   What will be the taste of grief?
            –   …………………
And we parted!

Sura:
The Nile flows quietly
      Seeping through the city's silence
            And the burning sorrows of villages.

Now friends no longer exchange greetings each morning
      No longer recognise each other.
            Everywhere one sees them, these one-time prophets,

Poverty-stricken, sipping their tea, their tears,
      Speechless.
            They hide death in their fraying clothes,

And all they can say to our children is: patience.
      They fade into the trees, commit suicide
            At night, derive from alcohol

Their arguments, embark on futile wars
      With their women, give up
            Their prayers, then disappear.

ثُمَّ يَنْتَحِلُونَ عَقْلَ زَجاجةِ الْخَمْرِ،
ويفتعلونَ حَرْباً في النساءِ،
ولا يقيمونَ الصَّلاةَ
ويرحلونْ.

تصعدُ الجدرانُ في اللبلابِ
والخرطومُ جالسةٌ على مقهىً تدخِّنُ
إستوى في اللَّيلِ قُطَّاعُ الطَّريقِ
وعابرو نصفَ المسافةِ
هل يكونُ الشارعُ الآن امتداداً
لاختناقِ اللَّيلِ بالعرباتِ والعُهرِ
وكنَّا عاشقَيْنِ، نفتِّش الأطفالَ
والأطفالُ في رئةِ المخابزِ

يسرقونَ النَّارَ
– ما اسْمي؟!
– أُسمِّيكِ احتراقَ الأرضِ، فانتفضي
– وما طعمُ الرَّمادِ؟!
– ... ...
إفترقنا!.

سورة:

الماءُ ضدَّ النَّارِ
والأمواجُ خارطةٌ تفرُّ من البلادْ
النَّارُ ضدَّ الماءِ
والدخان ذاكرةٌ تؤسِّسُ للرمادْ
الصَبِيَّةُ بين سِكِّيني وقلبي
والمدينةُ قبضةُ القمحِ

Walls climb the ivy
And Khartoum, sitting in a café
Smoking
In the dark you can't tell apart
Muggers from those whose journeys they'd cut short.
We were lovers, looking for our children
Who were breaking into bakeries, stealing fire
From the ovens' throats.

        — What name do you give me?
        — I call you earth's Fiery Anger
        — So rise up
        — What will be the taste of ashes?
        — ……………………..
        And we parted!

Sura:
Fire is the opposite of Water
And Smoke is a memory that prepares us only for ash.
Water is the opposite of Fire
And the waves are like maps, rippling across the land.
And the girl? She is somewhere between this heart and this knife. . .

City – you're a handful of grains of wheat, tucked
    Into the purses of usurers and slave-traders.
        And the black men

Are approaching, approaching. River Nile
    To what deserts are you taking my reflections? You depart
        And I stand among the horses, by your gate,

And my soul would embark on a holy journey too,
    For the silence suspended between us
        Is a language floating among the ruins of a beautiful,
            vanished past.

بحافظةِ المرابينَ وتجّارِ العبيدْ
والرِّجالُ السُّمْرُ يقتربون يقتربون
يا نيلُ ..
إلى أيِّ الصَّحارى
تحملُ الآن تصاويري وتمضي
وقفتي بين الجيادِ أمامَ بابِكَ
عُمْرَةٌ للرُّوح
والصَّمْتُ المعلَّقُ بيننا
لغةٌ من الزمنِ الجميلِ إلى الزمانِ المستحيلْ

يا أيها النيلُ – أَبي
هل كانت الأشجارُ نافذةً
لأحزانِ النساء
أم المرايا هشَّمت في الماءِ
تاريخَ الحضورِ الأنثويِّ
وثبَّتَتْ في العشبِ لونَ الفقر
إنَّ الفقرَ ينبُتُ في أراجيحِ الصِّغارِ
يورِّثُ الأطفالَ
صمتَ اللعنةِ الكبرى وكُفْرَ الأوَّلينْ.

سورة:

النيلُ يفتح ساعديه
يحدِّثُ الطيَّرَ المهاجرَ
ثم يصمُتُ
يعتلي عرشَ المكانِ
ولا ينامُ ..ولا ينامْ
النيل يَسْكَرُ بالنفاياتِ
ويَقْنَعُ بالمدينةِ وانكسارِ الليَّلِ

66

O River Nile, father
Were the trees merely windows reflecting women's sorrows,
Or have your waters shattered their images,
Drowned the history of women,
And painted forever their meadows the colour of poverty?
Poverty invades the children's playgrounds, leaving
Them silent, accursed, their heritage
Only anger and disbelief.

Sura:
The Nile opens his arms
Speaks to the migrant birds
        Falls silent
Reigns
      And never sleeps
      Never sleeps

The Nile drinks dry the desert's tavern,
Gets drunk on dumps of toxic waste,
Must survive in the city, falling apart
Each night, rising up through its history
      And never sleeps
      Never sleeps

The drums began with the sun
And its light filtered songs that entered into the pores of the soul.
In the river's shallows boats sheltered from toil and wind.
Now the carnivals of the blacks take fire
And the Nile has burst through the layers of time.

يصعدُ في الزَّمانِ

ولا ينامُ ..ولا ينامْ

طلعتْ من الشمس الطُّبولُ

ورقرقَ الضوءُ الغناءَ على مَسَامِ الرُّوح

والماءُ استراحاتُ المراكبِ من عناءِ الرِّيح

فجَّرَ النيلُ الزمانَ

وقد أطلَّتْ – فجأةً- مَرَوِي

ووجه العاشقِ النوبيِّ

إذْ يمشي على حزنِ السواقي

وهو يبحثُ في الجيادِ عن الرجولةِ

أين تبدأُ دورةُ الدَّمِ يا بعانخي

أين يحتدمُ النزيفُ

وأنت مستندٌّ على "كُوْشَ"

التي اهترأَتْ من الصمتِ المريْر

قل للجياد تحرَّكي ،

تَقِفُ المياهُ على أناملها

وتنشطرُ الخرائطُ هل تضيعُ الأرضُ،

والنيلُ اكتمالٌ للقرون القادمةْ؟!

النيلُ يعرفُ سوءةَ المدنِ التي ضاعتْ

ويعرفُ موقفَ الزَّمَنِ القَديم

ولا يحدِّثُ

إنه النيلُ

وللأجيالِ أن تمضي

وللأطفالِ أن يقفوا على الشَّطِّ طويلاً في انتظارِ العاقبة!

And, see, the city of Meroë appears
And the face of the Nubian lover
Who walks among the sorrows of the waterwheels
Searching for warriors among the horses.
Where does the line of ancestral blood begin
And when does the blood loss reach its climax,
O King Piankhy, enthroned ruler of Kush,
A kingdom unravelling in bitter silence?

Shout at the horses, and let
The waters ready themselves.
Let the maps explode. How can the land be lost
When the future belongs to the Nile?

The Nile knows of the disgrace of cities
That have vanished.
Knows of the old times
Yet never speaks.
It is the Nile. . .
Generations will pass, and there will always be children
Lingering on its banks,
Waiting
For it all to end.

Translated by Mark Ford and Hafiz Kheir

Meroe: Capital city of the ancient Sudanese Kingdom of Kush.
King Piankhy: Kushite king who conquered Egypt.

كأنَّما يروي عن مروي

كأنَّما صوت نقيقه يطلعُ من كسوتِه الحجريةْ
كأنَّما طبقات صوتِه تتلوَّنُ في الظلمةِ مغسولةً في طبقاتِ الأبديةْ

حينما رأيتُه ساهماً ووحيداً
في "فترينة" المتحفِ
تذكرتُ نطفتَه الأولى مختلطةً بطينتِه الأمِّ
كان يقنصُ الفرائسَ باللُّعابِ
يموِّهُ مفترسيه باللّونِ وأحابيلَ أخرى
يستيقظُ مثل أقرانه مِنْ سُباتِه الموسميٌّ
لموسم التزاوج الجديدْ
قبل أن يصبح أثراً غامضاً خلف الزجاجْ

كأنَّما يروي عن مروي
شاهداً على غروبِها مرةً ومرة على شموخٍ بمجدها..
كأنَّه في سُباتِه الأخيرِ يتأهبُ ثانيةً
للحياة بلباسٍ وتاجٍ جديدْ- بلسانٍ جديدْ.

70

He Tells Tales of Meroe

As if his croak sounds from stone itself
As if his voice in darkness is stained with the timbre of eternity

When I first saw him alone, lost in thought,
poised behind glass,
I recalled how his sperm had once spawned from the suck of
       motherly mud
to snatch prey with spit
A camouflaged trickster,
awakening each spring with his mates
to a spring of mating

Now an enigmatic relic behind glass,
perhaps he tells tales of Meroe –
witness to that city's sad trajectory from glory to dejection

In this, his last siesta,
he readies himself for life
with his new cloak, a new tongue and his crown

Translated by Sarah Maguire and Rashid El Sheikh

*Written during Al-Saddiq al-Raddi's residency at the Petrie Museum, this poem
was inspired by the figure of a crouching frog carved from hard fossiliferous limestone
in the museum's collection of items from Meroe. It was perhaps used to ensure the
fertility of the rains and the annual Nile flood (500 BCE to 100 CE).*

صُحْبَة مايكل انجلو

1

الملوكُ الذين مَضُوا ..
تركوا أثراً اسمه نسيانَهم
مثل (أليس) أو (كوش) ..إلخ .

تركوا: تيجاناً ممعنةً في غَرَابةٍ
بقايا هياكلَ عظميةٍ
رؤسَ أسماكَ – أسماءَ يَصْعُبُ نُطْقُها
مراودَ كُحلٍ – وصايا – مدائحَ منقوشةً على حجرٍ

بيدَ أنِّي تركتُكِ
أنتِ المُضاءَةُ بي
أينما حملتَكِ عروشُكِ
دماً طازجاً في شرايينَ تَفْنَى
و يصعبُ نسيانَكِ !

2

عند روما القديمةْ – أبوابَ روما القديمةْ
تصحبُني مُمْعِناً في صَرَامَةِ الدِّقَّة المتناهيةْ
لتصورك الخيطَ في ثقبه الأرْهَفَ
لتصورك الخطَّ والمنحنى
تصحبُني في صداقةِ الحجرْ
يدٌ ليدٍ
أصابعُ لأصابعَ
ثم ..
في مدخلِ الحانةِ
نقرعُ كأساً بكأسٍ
تضعُ النقطةَ التاليةْ

In the Company of Michelangelo

1

The kings who have gone
left us the remains of their forgettable names –
like al'Ais or Kush

They left us their peculiar crowns
shards of skeletons
fish-heads
unpronounceable words
kohl-sticks
commandments
and eulogies graven in stone

Yet I left you radiant,
resplendent, wherever your throne sets down
Live blood in mortal veins –
truly you are unforgettable

2

You accompany me
to the gates of ancient Rome
reaching the ends of perfection
as you envisage grace threading each tender aperture
as you envisage the faultless line, and the perfect circle

Let us be brothers in stone
hand in hand
fingers entwined –
and then,
on the threshold of a bar
we clink our glasses

في صفحةِ وجهٍ يتفرَّسُ تاريخَه

3

أينا المفتاحُ – عند بابكَ أو عند بابي ؟!

4

يَسْعَدُ الصمتُ

يَسْعَدُ الحال

يَسْعَدُ نُطْقُ الصورْ

كُلَّمَا تُرِكَ المقعدُ خالياً

كُلَّمَا تَوارَى صاحبُ المعطفِ

كُلَّمَا سُمعتْ شَهْقَةُ العَتْمَةِ الخفيفةِ

العناقُ – ميثولوجيا الحُضُورْ!

5

ما الحكمةُ ؟.. !؟

as you add the last touch
to a face already dreaming its history

3
Which of us is the key?
Your door or mine?

4
Silence is bliss
Life is bliss
Creation is bliss

Even though his chair is empty
even though he is gone
darkness is ablaze
with the presence of his embrace

5
What is the key?

Translated by Sarah Maguire and Sabry Hafez

al'Ais or Kush: Ancient Sudanese kingdoms

مفتاح الحياة

لابُدَّ مِنْ نَهرٍ لتنضجَ
لابدَّ مِنْ تميمةٍ ليسطعَ جوهرُها
لتكتملَ الأحجية!
الإلهُ- المَلِكُ أم المَلِكُ- الإلهُ؟!
أيهما السَّابقُ..
أيهما بيدِهِ مقبضَ البابِ
أو شفرة الأبديَّةِ؟!

... ...

السَّابقُ مازال لغزاً
كان تميمةً
مرآةً معدنيةً
مُذَّهباً أو مصقولاً بالنُّحاسِ
أيقونة شمسٍ بمدافنَ أَعْرَقُ
السَّابقُ بمجرى نَهرٍ سَابقْ!

76

The Key of Life

Civilisation springs from a river:
the brilliant glint of an amulet
permits this story to be told.
Who came first – a God or a King?
Who opens the door?
Who holds the key to the mystery of eternity?

...   ...

The firstborn is an enigma
            an amulet
                    a mirror
            fused from burnished copper
            an icon of the sun buried in a grave
a grave in a riverbed in the grave of a river

Translated by Sarah Maguire and Rashid El Sheikh

Written during Al-Saddiq Al-Raddi's residency at the Petrie Museum, this poem was inspired by a pottery offering-tray which has internal walls in the Meroitic form of the ancient Egyptian hieroglyph for the word 'ankh, meaning 'life' (500 BCE to 100 CE).

أثرُ امرأةٍ غريبة

1

الحارسُ يتعلَّقُ بـ الفانوسْ
الفارسُ بعُنْقِ الجَوادْ
نُوديتُ بـ الأُمِّ من كهفِ نَسْلٍ بعيدٍ
مِنْ حداءِ القوافلِ أو خوفِها
مِنْ صمتِها بَرَقَ الجُعْرانُ الذهبيِّ

العشيرةُ زادٌ وقِلادةٌ
المَسيرةُ وشمٌ
ودأبُ نجاةٍ على سِنٍّ رُمْح!

2

كلُّ ألفيةٍ، ثمة أنثى تَعْبُرُ "دَرْبَ الأربعينْ"
مُحَفَّلَةً في الغدوِّ أو الرواحِ
وقد لا تعودْ
كلُّ ألفيةٍ تَنْسَخُ أُخرى
... ...

ما تبقَّى: مَعْرفةٌ لم تَبُحْ بَعْدُ بأسرارِها
إناءٌ فخّاريٌّ- ثقبُهُ مِنْ أثرِ ألفيةٍ عَبَرتْ وتزيدُ
قلادةٌ منظومةٌ مِنْ صَدَفِ النّهرِ ومِنْ بحارٍ بعيدةٍ- فخارٌ ملوّنٌ بأكسيدِ النّحاسِ- قِشْرُ بيضِ النّعَامِ،..إلخ.
ما تبقَّى يَثِفُّ ويكشفُ!

3

رأسُ الحكمةِ
مزَّقَه رأسُ الخنجرْ..
... ...

78

Traces of an Unknown Woman

1
The watchman cleaves to his lantern.
The knight clings to the neck of his horse.
My name was passed down from mother to daughter –
like the songs sung by caravans to bolster their courage.
My name is the gleam of a golden scarab.

The tribe is both sustenance and a finely-wrought necklace.
The journey is like a tattoo.
Survival is balanced on the point of a spear.

2
Each millennium a woman journeyed along Darb Al Arbaien
Richly attired as she travelled the road back and forth.
She may not return.
Each millennium she starts out once more.

... ...

What remains: a ladle that keeps its own counsel.
A clay pot punctured by millennia.
A necklace of shells from distant seas, of shells gleaned from a far-off
    riverbed – pottery stained with the patina of copper – the blown
    egg of an ostrich, etc, etc.
What remains: revelation.

3
The fount of wisdom is pierced
by the point a dagger.

... ...

.. **في ذلك العصرْ** جَرَتْ وقائعُ كثيرةٌ كما رأى حفّارو مقابرْ. حُطِّمتْ معابدَ. حكى رجالٌ بأصابعَ يتطايرُ منها الشجرُ المحترقْ. نسوةٌ أيضاً شُوهدتْ أسرارهنّ لولا ضيقَ ذات اليدْ. جاء خُطّابُ العناصرِ جاءَ خطّاؤونَ كراريسُهم رُكِّبتْ جُمْلَةً على ناقةِ المَفسدَة. جرى تفحُّصُ السُلالاتِ بالعينِ المجرّدة- مُرِّغتْ أنوفُها. ألسنةٌ لا تُحصى جُعلتْ تحت حوافرِ الخيل. بطونٌ نُسبتْ لبطونْ.

An epoch of atrocities witnessed by the diggers of graves. Temples razed to the ground. Tales told by men whose fingers fire flames. Violated women branded by poverty, scorned with shame. Then came the discourse of separation and selection. Then came camp followers, wielding division, corrupt catalogues of sins straddled on camels, difference decreed by the naked eye. Numberless tongues were ripped out to be trammelled under the hooves of horses.

The end of a tribe is a tribe.

Translated by Sarah Maguire and Rashid El Sheikh

Written during Al-Saddiq al-Raddi's residency at the Petrie Museum, this poem was inspired by grave goods found in the isolated burial of a woman. These included two Nubian pottery vessels; a string of beads; a highly polished black silt scoop, of a form known from central Sudan; and a black-topped bowl with hole punched through it, perhaps to avoid recycling by the living. The items were found on the east bank of the Nile between Qau and Asyut in Middle Egypt. Here, desert roads connect the river valley west to the oases, east towards the Red Sea, and on both sides onward south to Sudan; the most famous of these routes is Darb Al Arbaien the 'Road of Forty Days', leading from Darfur in western Sudan to the Kharga Oasis and across to Asyut, which is still in use today. No other Nubian burial is recorded in this or any of the neighbouring cemeteries, but the desert foothills in the area sheltered some small, perhaps seasonal settlements of desert Nubians. The body of the woman was not recorded in detail, so her precise age and ethnicity are unknown, but those who buried her were following desert Nubian customs.

بعضُهنَّ يقيمُ عندك

بعضُهنَّ يلتقينَ بكَ
في زوايا الوجودِ المِعْتَمَةْ
بعضُهنَّ لا يضئنَ لي

بعضُهنَّ
يحملنَ ثأراتٍ ويُهْرَعَنَ
مُصْطَفِقَاتٍ بأوديةِ الروحْ

بعضُهنَّ تحت وطءِ الجبلْ
لا يحتمينَ بشَيْءْ
بعضُهنَّ مَلَكْنَ قلبَكَ
بعضُهنَّ ذَبْحَنَه
بعضُهنَّ كشفنَ عُرْيَكَ

بعضُهنَّ: أنا وأنتْ.

Some of Them Live with You

Some of them meet you
in the dark corners of the world
Some remain hidden

Some harbour revenge
or plot their escape
as they gallop down the valley of the wind

Some linger at the foot of a mountain
exposed to the elements

Some owned your heart
Some slaughtered it
Some stripped you naked

Some: me and you

Translated by Sarah Maguire and Atef Alshaer

نجمة

1

مَسَّني ضُوْءٌ
شَرَخَتْ زُجَاجَ أَحْلامِي
خَرَجْتُ مِنْ الفَضَاءْ

إِلَيَّ مِنْ بَعِيدٍ
تُعَبِّئُ نَجْمَةٌ تَعَبِي
تَعُجُّ إِلَيكِ حَجًّا عَامِراً
مِنْ الهَوَاءْ

وفِيَّ مِنْ خيوطٍ، كُوَّةٌ
خَضْرَاءُ، فيكِ
ولي خيلٌ – مِنْ الإِيحَاءِ
جُنْدٌ
مَنْ أَضَاءْ؟؟!

مَسَّني وخَرَجْتُ
هَشَّمْتُ البَيَاضَ كَتبتُ
خلفِي أُحْرِقَتْ كُتُبٌ
بَيَاضٌ مِزَقٌ
قَنَادِيلٌ سَوَادٌ
أَشْرَقَتْ في غَيِّها، سَدَرَتْ
بنفسجَةٌ على صَدْرِ السَّمَاءْ

2

يَتُّها النَّجْمَةُ السَّيِّدَةُ
على سَرِيرِكِ، قُرْبَ لُهَاثِ أَحْلامِكِ
عَنْ كَثَبٍ مِنْ مناديلِ عِطْرِكِ

84

A Star

1

Awoken by light, I scratch the glass
of dreams, and find myself
stepping free of shadows and silence.

In the distance a star was absorbing
my tiredness, and itself heading like a pilgrim
towards you, leaving blank its place in the heavens.

In the green pits of our being our inner
threads yearn; this radiance, that makes me feel I own
herds of horses, am as inspired as any knight –

what is its source? Shocked
into words, I defied the book-burners, the suffocators
of thought and feeling, all who'd censor and shroud knowledge.

And a violet blossomed fiercely in the bosom of the sky.

2

Star Woman,
the memory of our embrace still lives
in this bed, adjacent to your dreams
and desires, and near these handkerchiefs
drenched in your scent.

"بِالضَّبْطِ"

السَّاعَةَ الثَّالِثَةَ – الفَجْرَ

بعد نُهوضِكِ مُرْبَّحَةً بِبقايا نُعاسٍ مُهاجِرٍ

وأرَقٍ لا يُقِيمْ

تَسْكُنُ – تَحْتَ المِلاءَةِ

ذِكْرَى عِناقٍ له شَخِيرُكِ الهادِئُ

وهو يُؤَكِّدُ بَوحَكِ للنوم

بالقَلَقِ تُجَاهَ حنينِكِ فيهِ للمرآةْ

تَسْكُنُ نُطْفَةُ نُورٍ

مِنْ جَسَدٍ أَلَّهَ صَبْوَتَهُ

في العُمْرِ، وسَمَّى ما سَمَّى

تَسْكُنُ تَحْتَ الوِسَادَةِ رَائِحَةٌ خَضْرَاءُ

تَخُصُّكِ فِيَّ

وتَسْكُنُ عَائِلَةُ الأَسْمَاءِ النُّورِيَّةُ

للشَّيْءِ الغَامِضِ

تَسْكُنُ سَيِّدَةُ الأَسْمَاءْ

تَسْكُنُ سَيِّدَةُ الأَشْيَاءْ

You woke in the dawn
at three exactly, drowsing,
still dazed …
Beneath the sounds of your breathing
lurks a worry: where is your mirror?
And this droplet of light
reflecting a passion
that found a name for everything…

Under the pillows also, an aroma
alive and ours – and the long list
of names we have bestowed
on this affair. Surely
a goddess lives there too, the one
who knows the names of all things.

Translated by Mark Ford and Hafiz Kheir

تَنْقِيطْ

يَسْجِنُ نَفْسَه في وَرَقَةٍ بَيْضَاءْ
يَفْتَحُ فيها وَطناً لامرَأةٍ
تَفْتَحُ فِيه العَالَمْ
يُضيءُ مِنْ عَالَمٍ لا يَدَّعِيهْ
مِنْ عَالَمٍ يشْتَهِيهْ
يَسْكُنُ فيهْ

Writing

He has trapped himself in a blank page.
He creates a home in it
for a woman
who unwraps there his own
inner world. He glows
in this world he aches for
and lives in,
yet which is not his.

Translated by Mark Ford and Hafiz Kheir

أنتَ مِنهُم ؟!

ليس كثيراً ما أُهْتَمُّ

إلاَّ بامرأةٍ طعمُها لا يكادُ يُرى

إلاَّ بِمَنْ يُتْبِعُ الخطوةَ

إلاَّ بنفسي – أراني

أَتَجَسَّدُ في الأشياءِ

أُروحُ بينَها كالهائمِ في ذِكْرى

أقتربُ من حَدْسِ الخروجِ

. . . .

ما رأيْتُ مَرَاكِبَ في زينةٍ

تُبهِجُ ليلَ العينِ

رؤوسَ أشجارٍ – إلاَّ من العتمةِ

ما سكَنْتُ إلى طيفِ عِطْرٍ

وما بقِيْتُ على خاطرٍ

. . . .

سُوقٌ عظيمةٌ

تَبْلَغُ صوتَ الفأسِ

صمتٌ بَلَغَ الجُذُورْ

النَّملُ لا يهتمُّ بامرأةٍ

تحرقُ تاريخَها بينما تُوْلَدُ

مَنْ أضاءَكَ يا ماضي

يُضيِءُكَ يا قَادِمُ

لا يحرقُ المراكبَ أو يُلَوِّثُ القلوبْ؟!.

Are You the One?

I only notice
a women who attracts no notice
a woman who follows the path
I take

Reincarnated, mirrored in visions,
I wander through images, drifting on memories,
intuiting exodus

I'm blind to those ornamental boats
fashioned for attention
The roof of the trees is lost in darkness
I seek rest only in fragrance
And no one remembers me

A great souk
swallows the sound of an axe
with a silence that strikes to the roots

No one notices a woman
who burns her past while being born anew

Who can illuminate history?
Will the one who is leaving
set the future alight?
Will the one who is coming
burn those boats
and tarnish your heart?

Translated by Sarah Maguire and Sabry Hafez

تماثيل الحدائق

الليلة الأخيرة ...

الليلة الأولى ...

... بينهما البحيرة الصافيةْ

....

تركتَ كأس الذكرى للذكرى

تنظم ذراته ذهب الليلات- جميعاً

تركتَ صوته- علي فاركا توري- بمطلقه

يسبحُ

في فضَّةِ الغرفة

المفروشة بلآلئ الساعات والدقائقْ

تركتَ الحصانَ الخشبيّ الصغيرْ

الدبَّ القطنيَ على الكرسيُّ

الحدائقَ في الجوارِ

الشمسَ تمرحُ في الثامنةِ مساءً

تركتَ نافذةً مشرعةً

صباحاً يلبسُ زيَّ صباحْ

تركتَ الزهرةَ تكدحُ كدحاً

فتلاقيه ..

تركته- عمداً:

الطاؤوس يعملُ- مأسوراً- في حقل الجمالْ

... ...

لم يَعُدْ- ما تبقَّى من الوقتِ..

.. من ليلته تلك..

لم تَعُدْ اليواقيتُ ..

لم يَعُدْ الظمأُ من ألقِ الشراعْ

بينما عدتَ مُلتهماً- كاملاً

Garden Statues

The last night…
the first night…
… between them the clarity of an untroubled lake
…. ….

You left that glass of memory to memory –
    let its essence transmute all these nights into gold

You left the voice of Ali Farka Touré
    soaring
    through the silvered light of a room,
    a room inlaid with the jewels of minutes and hours

You left your hands lost in the familiar characters of a vanishing keyboard

You left a wooden rocking horse
    an old teddy bear propped on a chair
    the neighbouring gardens

You left the sun still toying with the sky at eight in the evening

You left a window open
    on a morning arrayed with morning

You left a flower labouring towards morning

You deliberately left that peacock arrested in the field of beauty

…. …. ….

Whatever time is left of that night
    will never return…

من التجربةٌ

من صدفٍ

من فخارٍ – بلا زخرف

عادثْ الأيامُ – بلا هدايا

عادثْ وصاياكَ

عادَ السكونْ!

These jewels will never return
A sail will never quench its thirst for the horizon

And when you left
        you were cast in the bronze of that experience
        you were consumed and yet complete
        you were fashioned from mother-of-pearl
        you were made of unadorned clay

Weekdays returned, empty handed
Routine returned

And silence reigned

Translated by Sarah Maguire and Sabry Hafez

ثعلبٌ صغير

ثعلبٌ صغيرٌ
يمرحُ في قلبكِ الملوَّث
أفلحَ في الهطول تلك الليلةْ
وجهُكِ
غمرَهُ بالصعلكةِ واليُتمْ..
بما يكفي ويفيضْ..

تلك الليلة أوحشتْ ممرَّكِ الأثير نَحْوي
أوحشتكِ كثيراً
أوحشتْ قَمَراً يتعلَّمُ الأسْماء
فلم نَعُدْ بحاجةٍ لإناءٍ يتكسَّرُ
إثرَ رقصةِ السنحابْ
وتَعَلُّق الظُّلْمَةِ بآخِرِ قَطَراتِ النبيذْ

عنِّي: ظَمِلتُ بالظمأ
يدي أَرعشَتْهَا رَغْبَةُ الحُنُوِّ
وما مِنْ ثعلبٍ آخرَ في الطريقْ!

Small Fox

Suddenly – a small fox, playful,
floods your wounded heart with joy
He searches your face with his singular gaze,
knows you're at one with his vagabond stance

That very night I longed for you,
I missed your exquisite arousal,
I yearned for that moon we named together
After the squirrel had slipped off,
we needed nothing
but night, and the last dregs of wine

And as for me – I am drunk with thirst,
I am shaking with desire for you –
but here there's not a fox to be found

Translated by Sarah Maguire and Sabry Hafez

سطوع

يَقُلْنَ إِنَّهُنَّ أَصْغَرُ مِنِّي
ويَمْضِينَ مُسْرِعاتٍ في وداعي
يَقْتَفِينَ أَثَرَ النُّبُوءَةِ الكاذبة
وأنا أتوارَى من الحنانِ دامعاً
قربَ حائطٍ يتكسَّرُ
من لَذَّةٍ مبهمةْ

إِسْرِعي في التَّماثُلِ
في التَزيِّي بأوراقِ الخديعة
وراءَ تَلِّ الحُدُوسْ

تَعَلَّقي بِهِنَّ وتابعيني
من وراءِ الوضوحِ المتَواري

مثلَ صائدٍ تُحْرثِينَ الظِّلالَ الرَّهيفةَ
في اللَّيلِ، تَسْلَخِينَ الدَّمعةَ
من صَمْغِ الحاقِنِ الدَّمْعَ
في نَجمةٍ تُحْرُسُهُ
خلفَ بابِ الوجودْ!.

98

Radiance

They say they're too young for me
They see right through me
and brush me off with coy excuses
Tearful, I retreat
behind a wall eroded by longing

Race to resemble them –
dress in deceit
disavow insight

Follow them
and I will be revealed –
a hunter quarrying the translucent shadows

At night you will see tears
seep from a ringed star
fixed at the ends of existence

Translated by Sarah Maguire and Atef Alshaer

رفقة

مَنْ يَصِفُكِ ويقولْ
يحرجني/ لذلك في حضورِكِ
أفتحُ عيني على آخرها
وأغلقُ فمي
مُتكتِّماً على غيابك السرِّي

(.. فَمُكِ المليءُ بالرغبةْ
عيناكِ الطافحتانِ بالحنانْ
جسدُك الذي يَرعَشُ
وهو يدعو ..)

أولُ مَنْ يَصِفُ الحياةَ
يحرجني لذلك أغشاكِ كلَّ ظهيرةٍ
لأقصَّ الغَسَقْ

أنتِ ..
أنتِ ..
أحقُّ بالإيمانْ !

Sympathy

I wince
whenever your name comes up
All ears, I seal my lips
keeping your secret a secret

(. . . Your mouth is ripe with desire
your eyes brim with tenderness
your body trembles as it calls . . .)

Anyone who mentions you cuts me to the quick,
and so I come to you in the heat of the noon
to whisper the story of dawn

You . . .
You . . .
My only creed!

Translated by Sarah Maguire and Atef Alshaer

تَوق

يَعْرِفُ كيفَ يُشْعِلُ مَسَاءَاتِهِ
ويُضيْءُ صَبَاحَاتِهِ
كان يُشْعِلُهَا بالعَرَقْ
ويُضيئُهَا بالغِنَاءْ

مُتَوَرِّداً
يَضَعُ الغِنَاءَ أَمَامَ صُنْدُوقِ السَّجَائِرِ
يُشْعِلُ امْرَأَةً
ومِرْآةً
وأُمْسِيَةً
ويُشْرِقُ في الدُّخَانْ

مُتَفَحِّماً
يَجِدُ الأغَانِي خَلْفَ بَارُودِ الثَوانِي
.. يُطْفِئُ العُمْرَ ... .. ويَمْضِي
خَافِقاً بالهَجْرِ والتُّوْقِ
مُرَفْرِفاً بالرِّيحِ
.... يَمْضِي
صَوبَ نَجْمَتِهِ البَعِيدَةْ

Longing

He knows how to light up his evenings
and brighten his mornings:
once, he would ignite her with sweat,
once, he would burnish her with song

Flushed,
he graces his cigarettes with an ode
He enflames a woman,
a mirror,
and a night –
as he rises through his cloud of smoke

Burnt,
he finds songs in the barrel of time
. . . . he snuffs out time. . . . and moves on
He longs for travel and freedom
Borne by the wind
. . . . . . he journeys
to his distant star

Translated by Sarah Maguire and Atef Alshaer

ظهيرةٌ كسولةٌ
تقودني من طيوفكِ إلى كوب الشاي
إلى عناق الحيرةِ
وفقَ مزاجٍ صاخبٍ بالفضولْ
أتحسَّسُ قاعَ الرائحةِ
التي تبقى
من حضوركِ
أحدسُ لوناً يُضيئُكِ من الظلِّ
وبقايا الأقاصيصِ عنكِ
يا خاطئةْ
كالرسولة من دهنِ الأحاديث تنسلِّينَ
من فواكه الرائحة الناعسةْ
وتسيِّجينَ الخواطرَ بأصنافِ البداهاتْ

Only

A lazy noon
stirs me from your memory to this glass of tea
and a wondering embrace

In a mood busy with inquisitiveness
I smell the lees of the scent
that lingers
behind you

I sense your shade in the shadows
in the dregs of all that gossip –
Oh you sinner!

Like a rumoured prophet's advent
you slide from the ripe fruit of sleep
afire with ideas, your flashing wit

Translated by Sarah Maguire and Sabry Hafez

أُغنية

ماثلٌ للرِّيحِ
في قبعةٍ لا تُخْفِي
بمعطفٍ يلتفُّ – على عمودِ الغبارْ
النَّحيلُ

يَرَى فضاءً
ولا يقطفُ وردةً
حتى يَرَاك

(بالممرِّ الضَّيِّقِ
بين أكوامِ الزِّبالةِ
يُشْهِرُ منقارَهُ
ويضربُ بالأجنحة).

Song

Facing downwind in a dust storm
wrapped up in his cloak
and wearing a hat that can't make him vanish –

this skinny man
scans the horizon
gathering – but not quite yet – flowers
until the moment you meet

(. . . but stuck in this alleyway
among mountains of rubbish
he longs to lift up his beak
unfurl his wings
and take flight . . .)

Translated by Sarah Maguire and Hafiz Kheir

لهاثٌ

كأنَّها تَقتربُ من البابِ
تسمعُ دقات قلبِكَ
أو
كأنك في انتظارِها
تَحْضُرُ طيورُ الضُّحى
وتَصْطَفُّ على النافذةُ
....
ساعةٌ من الصَّبرِ
غابةٌ من الهديلِ والشقشقةْ.

Breathless

Your heart thumps –
as if she were already
at your door.

Or – as if expecting her –
all the birds in the midday sky
arrive to clamour at your window.

. . . .

An age of patience.
A forest of fluttering.

Translated by Sarah Maguire and Hafiz Kheir

عَرشْ

مَرْفُوعَةٌ
عَلَى أَصَابِعَ وَلا أَصَابِعَ للمَوْجِ
مَدْلُوقَةٌ
على النَّهْرِ ولا قَامَةَ للمَوْجِ○

في الثَّانِيَةِ الرَّهِيفَةِ
بين أَنْ تَصْعَدَ وتَسِيحْ
تَخْلِقُ العَالَمَ
تَمْحُو رَسْمَهُ
دون أَنْ تَسْتَرِيحْ!!

Throne

Aloft
as though lifted on fingertips –
and yet waves have no fingers
Her desire
structures the water –
and yet waves have no structure

In the split second
between crest and collapse
the world is created
and the world is annulled
without end

Translated by Sarah Maguire and Atef Alshaer

صَلاةٌ

بين حِبْرٍ ودَمْعَةٍ
تَسْجُدُ الكَلِمَةُ – رَافِعَةُ الرَأْسِ
تَرْفَعُ الدُّعَاءَ بِنَفْسِهَا
وتُزَخْرِفُ الأُورَاقْ!!

Prayer

Between ink and a tear
The Word is prostrated – with its head held high
It evokes its own divinity
It illuminates the page

Translated by Sarah Maguire and Atef Alshaer

Al-Saddiq Al-Raddi is widely regarded as one of the leading African poets writing in Arabic. Famous since a teenager, he is admired for the lyric intensity of his poetry and for his principled opposition to Sudan's dictatorship. His *Collected Poems* was published in 2010. A distinguished journalist, he was forced into exile in 2012 and now lives in London.

Sarah Maguire is the founder and director of the Poetry Translation Centre and editor of the anthology *My Voice: A Decade of Poems from the Poetry Translation Centre* (Bloodaxe Books, 2014). Author of four highly praised poetry collections, her selected poems *Almost the Equinox*, was published by Chatto & Windus in 2015.

Mark Ford has published three collections of poetry, *Landlocked* (1992), *Soft Sift* (2001), and *Six Children* (2011). He has also written a biography of the French poet, playwright and novelist, Raymond Roussel, and translated Roussel's *New Impressions of Africa*. He teaches in the English Department at University College London.

Atef Alshaer is a Lecturer in Arabic Language and Culture at the University of Westminster. His many publications include the books *Poetry and Politics in the Modern Arab World* and *Language and National Identity in Palestine: Representations of Power and Resistance in Gaza*. He was educated at Birzeit University in Palestine and at SOAS where he obtained his PhD and taught for a number of years.

Hafiz Kheir was born 1968 in Khartoum and moved to the UK in 1992. A translator and filmmaker, he graduated from the Film & Television School at the London Institute in 2000. He studied drama and theatre from 1982 to 1986 at the Youth Palace, Omdurman.

Rashid El Sheikh migrated from Sudan to the UK in 1991 as a political refugee. He obtained a diploma in International Studies from Birkbeck College and an MA in Cultural Policy Management from City University. He is Senior Coordinator of the International Relations Department at the Wellington Hospital in London.

Sabry Hafez is Distinguished Professor of Comparative Literature at Qatar University and Emeritus Professor of Modern Arabic and Comparative Literature at SOAS. He is Editor-in-Chief of the online journal, *Al-Kalimah*. His many publications have made a significant contribution to the discipline of world literature studies.